ABOUT HABITATS

Grasslands

To the One who created grasslands.
—*Genesis* 1:1

Published by
PEACHTREE PUBLISHERS
1700 Chattahoochee Avenue
Atlanta, Georgia 30318-2112
www.peachtree-online.com

Text © 2011 by Cathryn P. Sill
Illustrations © 2011 by John C. Sill

Illustrations created in watercolor on archival quality 100% rag watercolor paper.
Text and titles set in Novarese from Adobe.

Printed in Singapore
10 9 8 7 6 5 4 3 2
Printed and manufactured in February 2013 by Imago in Singapore

Library of Congress Cataloging-in-Publication Data

Sill, Cathryn P., 1953-
  About habitats : grasslands / written by Cathryn Sill; illustrated by
John Sill. -- 1st ed.
    p. cm.
  ISBN 13: 978-1-56145-559-1 / ISBN 10: 1-56145-559-8
  1. Grasslands--Juvenile literature.
  2. Grassland ecology--Juvenile literature. I. Sill, John, ill. II. Title.
  QH87.7.S55 2011
  577.4--dc22
                    2010026690

ABOUT HABITATS

Grasslands

Written by **Cathryn Sill** Illustrated by **John Sill**

PEACHTREE
ATLANTA

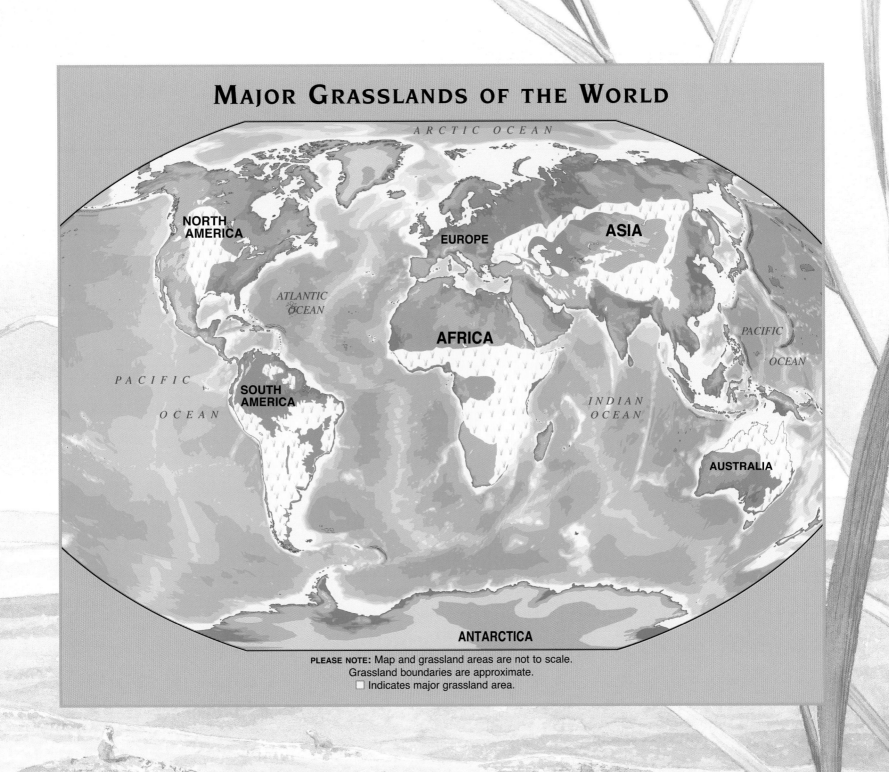

MAJOR GRASSLANDS OF THE WORLD

ARCTIC OCEAN

NORTH
AMERICA

EUROPE

ASIA

*ATLANTIC
OCEAN*

AFRICA

*PACIFIC

OCEAN*

SOUTH
AMERICA

*PACIFIC

OCEAN*

*INDIAN
OCEAN*

AUSTRALIA

ANTARCTICA

PLEASE NOTE: Map and grassland areas are not to scale.
Grassland boundaries are approximate.
☐ Indicates major grassland area.

Grasslands

Grasslands are large open places where most of the plants are grasses.

The grasses may be short, tall, or mixed.

Wildflowers grow in some grasslands.

PLATE 3
TALLGRASS PRAIRIE

Regal Fritillary

A few trees and shrubs are found
in other grasslands.

Some grasslands have hot summers
and cold winters.

Others are hot all year.

PLATE 6
SAVANNA

Giant Anteater

Grasslands have times of rain followed by long periods of dry weather.

Fire is important to grasslands. It burns away old parts of plants so new ones can grow.

Many animals that live in grasslands eat
the leaves of grass.

Some animals eat grass seeds.

Others hunt and eat the grass-eaters.

PLATE 11
PAMPAS

Maned Wolf

Some grassland animals stay safe
by living in large herds.

PLATE 12
SAVANNA

Common Zebra
Blue Wildebeest
Lion

Many are fast runners since there are
few places to hide from enemies.

PLATE 13
SAVANNA

Ostrich

Some grassland animals are able to hide
in the grass.

PLATE 14
STEPPE

Eurasian Skylark

Others stay safe in underground burrows.

PLATE 15
SHORTGRASS PRAIRIE

American Badger

Grasslands provide food for people
all over the world.

PLATE 16
Bread made from grains
grown in grasslands

Grasslands are important places that
need to be protected.

Afterword

PLATE 1

Grasslands are dry places that get more rain than deserts but not enough rain for forests to grow. They are found on every continent except Antarctica. Grasslands cover about one-fourth of the land on Earth. American Bison (also called buffalo) are the largest land animal in North America. Huge herds of American Bison once grazed on the grasslands of North America. They were almost hunted to extinction in the late 1800s. American Bison are now protected and their numbers have slowly increased.

PLATE 2

Grasslands in North America are called prairies. Shortgrass prairies are dry grasslands with short, scattered grass plants. Western Rattlesnakes sometimes live in burrows made by other animals found in shortgrass prairies. Prairies with more rainfall have taller, thicker grasses. The grasses in these tallgrass prairies may grow up to 8 feet tall (2.4 meters). White-tailed Deer are common in a variety of habitats, including tallgrass prairies. Mixed-grass prairies have both tall and short grasses. Upland Sandpipers are shorebirds that live in this type of open grassland.

PLATE 3

Grasses are the most common plants in grasslands, but other plants may grow there. Insects such as bees and butterflies eat nectar from the prairie wildflowers. Regal Fritillaries live in tallgrass prairies on the Great Plains of North America. These butterflies are becoming rare in many areas because of habitat destruction.

PLATE 4

Grasslands scattered with trees and shrubs are called savannas. African savannas are home to many grassland animals. White Rhinoceroses, the second largest land animals, have wide square lips that help them graze on grass. Giraffes eat leaves from the trees that grow on the savannas. Impalas feed on green grass during the growing season and on woody plants when the grass is not growing.

PLATE 5

Temperate grasslands have hot summers and cold winters. In Eurasia these grasslands are called steppes. Saigas are antelopes that live on dry Eurasian steppes. Their large, drooping noses may help filter out dust in summer and warm the air they breathe in winter. The antelopes' coats are reddish brown in summer and nearly white in winter. Saigas are endangered because of illegal hunting and habitat destruction.

PLATE 6

Tropical grasslands are located near the equator. They have hot weather year-round. These grasslands have two seasons: the rainy season and the dry season. Giant Anteaters live in grasslands and forests in South and Central America. They eat mostly ants and termites. Giant Anteaters use their strong front legs and large claws to dig into the nests of ants and termites. They lap up the insects with their long sticky tongues.

PLATE 7

Rainfall in temperate grasslands usually comes in late spring and early summer. Some temperate grasslands may get snow in winter. The rainy season in tropical grasslands lasts several months. All grasslands have periods of drought following the rain. To help grasses survive the long spells without rain, the plants stop growing during the dry times.

PLATE 8

Lightning often causes fires in grasslands. Grasses are able to survive fires because even if the upper part of the plant burns, the parts that grow underground are not affected by the heat. Frequent fires in grasslands keep most trees and other large plants from growing there. Animals survive grassland fires by running away or hiding in underground burrows. European White Storks and other grassland birds sometimes hunt at the edge of fires. They snatch up insects and other small animals that are trying to escape the flames. European White Storks live in Eurasia and Africa.

PLATE 9

Grasses grow from the base or bottom of their leaves. This allows the plants to keep growing after grazing animals clip off the ends. Some small animals such as grasshoppers eat grass one leaf at a time. Others eat large amounts of grass as they graze. Different kinds of animals eat different parts of the grass plants. This ensures that the grass can feed many animals. Ebony Grasshoppers, Black-tailed Prairie Dogs, and Pronghorns (one of the fastest mammals in the world) live in grasslands of North America.

PLATE 10

Important nutrients in grass seeds help many grassland animals survive. Some animals search for seeds that have fallen to the ground. Others take seeds right off the plants. Budgerigars (also called parakeets) are small parrots that live in huge flocks in Australian grasslands. They often fly long distances to search for seeds. Budgerigars are popular pets.

PLATE 11

Some grassland predators are big enough to hunt large grazers. Smaller predators hunt for prey such as insects. Maned Wolves, the largest members of the wild dog family in South America, hunt small animals including mammals, birds, reptiles, and insects. Their long legs may help them see over tall grass. The wolves also eat fruit and other parts of plants.

PLATE 12

Because there aren't many places for large animals to hide on grasslands, they often move around together in herds when they are looking for food and water. In large groups, there are more pairs of eyes and ears watching or listening for danger, so predators have a harder time sneaking up on them. Lions often hunt Common Zebras and Blue Wildebeests on African savannas.

PLATE 13

Some grassland animals are able to run fast for long periods of time. Ostriches can run over 30 miles per hour (50 kilometers per hour) for half an hour and reach speeds over 43 miles per hour (70 kilometers per hour) for short distances. They run from predators because they cannot fly. Ostriches are the largest birds in the world. They live in Africa.

PLATE 14

Many grassland animals are able to hide from enemies or prey because they are camouflaged. Eurasian Skylarks' feathers are the same colors as the grasses they live among. Their homes are camouflaged, too. They build grass nests on the ground, where they are often hidden among plants. Eurasian Skylarks live in open habitats in Eurasia and northern Africa.

PLATE 15

Underground burrows provide animals with places where they can hide from predators, store food, sleep, and raise babies. The burrows also provide shelter in very hot or very cold weather. American Badgers have strong front legs and sharp claws that are good for digging. When in danger, American Badgers can dig holes very quickly. They have several burrows or dens in their home range. American Badgers live in North America.

PLATE 16

Most of the crops grown all over the world are types of grasses. Much of the farmland in the world was once grassland. Grasses that provide food for people include wheat, corn, rice, oats, and sugarcane. People use grass seeds to make breads and cereals. Grassland animals provide people with milk and meat.

PLATE 17

For thousands of years people all over the world have used grasslands for grazing domestic animals and planting crops. Many grasslands have been destroyed. It is important for people to restore and protect grasslands. Careful management will allow grasslands to continue providing homes for wildlife and food for people. Lesser Prairie-Chickens of North America have become rare because of habitat destruction.

GLOSSARY

BIOME—an area such as a grassland or wetland that shares the same types of plants and animals
ECOSYSTEM—a community of living things and their environment
HABITAT—the place where animals and plants live

Burrow—a hole in the ground dug by an animal
Camouflage—colors or patterns on an animal that help it hide
Drought—a period of time with little or no rain
Equator—an imaginary line around the center of the earth halfway between the North and South Poles
Graze—to feed on growing grass
Nectar—a sweet liquid formed in flowers
Prey—an animal that is hunted and eaten by a predator
Shorebird—a bird such as a sandpiper or a plover that lives in shoreline habitats and open country
Shrub—a low woody plant smaller than a tree; a bush
Temperate—referring to a mild climate where the weather is not very hot and not very cold
Tropical—referring to the area near the equator that is hot year-round

BIBLIOGRAPHY

BOOKS

AMERICA'S PRAIRIES AND GRASSLANDS: GUIDE TO PLANTS AND ANIMALS by Marianne D. Wallace (Fulcrum Publishing)
A TRUE BOOK: GRASSLANDS by Darlene R. Stille (Children's Press)
EXPLORE THE GRASSLANDS by Kay Jackson (Capstone Press)
FIRST REPORTS: GRASSLANDS by Susan H. Gray (Compass Point Books)
SAVANNAS: LIFE IN THE TROPICAL GRASSLANDS by Laurie Peach Toupin (Franklin Watts)
THE WIDE OPEN GRASSLANDS: A WEB OF LIFE by Philip Johansson (Enslow Publishers)

WEBSITES

http://www.blueplanetbiomes.org/grasslands.htm
http://library.thinkquest.org/11353/ecosystems.htm
http://www.mbgnet.net/
http://www.nhptv.org/natureworks/nwep8d.htm

ABOUT... SERIES

ISBN 978-1-56145-234-7 HC
ISBN 978-1-56145-312-2 PB

ISBN 978-1-56145-038-1 HC
ISBN 978-1-56145-364-1 PB

ISBN 978-1-56145-028-2 HC
ISBN 978-1-56145-147-0 PB

ISBN 978-1-56145-301-6 HC
ISBN 978-1-56145-405-1 PB

ISBN 978-1-56145-256-9 HC
ISBN 978-1-56145-335-1 PB

ISBN 978-1-56145-207-1 HC
ISBN 978-1-56145-232-3 PB

ISBN 978-1-56145-141-8 HC
ISBN 978-1-56145-174-6 PB

ISBN 978-1-56145-358-0 HC
ISBN 978-1-56145-407-5 PB

ISBN 978-1-56145-331-3 HC
ISBN 978-1-56145-406-8 PB

ISBN 978-1-56145-488-4 HC

ISBN 978-1-56145-454-9 HC

ISBN 978-1-56145-183-8 HC
ISBN 978-1-56145-233-0 PB

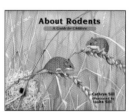

ISBN 978-1-56145-454-9 HC

ABOUT HABITATS SERIES

ISBN 978-1-56145-390-0 HC
ISBN 978-1-56145-636-9 PB

ISBN 978-1-56145-559-1 HC

ISBN 978-1-56145-469-3 HC

ISBN 978-1-56145-432-7 HC
ISBN 978-1-56145-689-5 PB

ISBN 978-1-56145-618-5 HC

THE SILLS

Cathryn Sill, a former elementary school teacher, is the author of the acclaimed ABOUT... series. With her husband John and her brother-in-law Ben Sill, she coauthored the popular bird-guide parodies, A FIELD GUIDE TO LITTLE-KNOWN AND SELDOM-SEEN BIRDS OF NORTH AMERICA, ANOTHER FIELD GUIDE TO LITTLE-KNOWN AND SELDOM-SEEN BIRDS OF NORTH AMERICA, and BEYOND BIRDWATCHING.

John Sill is a prize-winning and widely published wildlife artist who illustrated the ABOUT... series and illustrated and coauthored the FIELD GUIDES and BEYOND BIRDWATCHING. A native of North Carolina, he holds a B.S. in Wildlife Biology from North Carolina State University.

The Sills live in Franklin, North Carolina.